LIVING LANGUAGE®

Learn Spanish Anywhere

AN ACTIVITY KIT FOR KIDS AND GROWN-UPS

Activities by
Marie-Claire Antoine

Spanish by
Nancy Noguera

Edited by
Helga Schier, Ph.D.

LIVING LANGUAGE®, A RANDOM HOUSE COMPANY
NEW YORK

Published in the United States by Living Language, A Random House Company

www.livinglanguage.com

Interior Design: Jesse Cohen
Illustrations: Chie Ushio

ISBN: 1-4000-2302-5
ISBN-13: 978-1-4000-2302-8

Library of Congress Cataloging-in-Publication Data
Antoine, Marie-Claire.
    Learn Spanish together : an activity kit for kids and grown-ups / activities by Marie-Claire Antoine ;
Spanish by Nancy Noguera ; edited by Helga Schier. — 1st ed.
        p.   cm. — (Living Language)
    1. Spanish language—Study and teaching (Primary)—English speakers—Activity programs.
2. Creative activities and seat work.   I. Noguera, Nancy.   II. Schier, Helga.   III. Title.
IV. Series: Living Language parent/child activity kit.
PC4066.A77   1999
468.2'421—dc21   99-19112
                                                                             CIP

This book is available at special discounts for bulk purchases for sales promotions or premiums. Special editions, including personalized covers, excerpts of existing books, and corporate imprints, can be created in large quanti-ties for special needs. For more information, write to Special Markets/Premium Sales, 1745 Broadway, MD 6-2, New York, New York 10019 or e-mail specialmarkets@randomhouse.com.

PRINTED IN CHINA

10 9 8 7 6 5 4 3 2 1

Contents

Appendixes   40

Introduction

Learn Spanish Anywhere is a fun and effective program for kids and grown-ups that teaches essential Spanish vocabulary and phrases through sixteen exciting, childproof, and easy-to-prepare indoor activities. Whether you already speak Spanish and want to teach your children or you want to learn along with them, whether you're a parent looking for at-home entertainment or a teacher looking for additional classroom activities, this program offers great educational fun and entertainment for kids and grown-ups alike. In "Home Planets" your kids will learn the rooms of the house, in "Dice Man" they'll learn how to count, in "Find the Rainbow" they'll learn the colors, and in "Let's Find a Disguise" they'll learn the names for basic clothing items—all in Spanish!

The complete **Living Language® Learn Spanish Together** fun pack includes three book-and-CD sets (Learn in the Kitchen, Learn in the Car, and Learn Anywhere); three sheets of color stickers, one sheet for each program; and a box of crayons. The book contains a step-by-step description of all sixteen activities, a two-way glossary, and a translation of all songs and rhymes used on the recordings. At the beginning of each activity, carefully read the instructions, and gather all the materials necessary to complete the activity. During the activity, follow the step-by-step instructions carefully. Start the CD to listen to the two narrators as they guide you through singing Spanish folk songs, creating a fun Halloween mask, hosting your own TV show, and playing a game of "Simon Says." Without even noticing it, you will learn the most essential Spanish words and phrases. Sugges-tions for adapting and modifying the activity to enhance learning conclude every activity.

The book doubles as a scrapbook that the kids can personalize with drawings, photographs, or the included stickers to create a record of the completed activities.

The appendix features a two-way glossary that will prove to be an invaluable reference tool. In addition to all vocabulary used during the program, the glossary includes several thematic vocabulary lists that go beyond the scope of this program.

The recordings feature vocabulary, phrases, songs, and rhymes, while the two narrators, Lola and Juan, lead you gently through each activity. They will teach the vocabulary and phrases and provide ample opportunity for you to practice your pronunciation. Just listen and repeat, and soon you'll be speaking Spanish on your own. Spanish songs and rhymes help with learning. Don't worry if it seems difficult to follow the songs the first time around. Just listen to them again. For your convenience, transcriptions and translations of the songs and rhymes are included in the appendix of the book.

And now, let's begin. *¡Ahora, vamos a empezar!*

Activities

Time: 30 minutes

Vocabulary and Phrases: Rooms of the House

la casa house • *la cocina* kitchen • *la sala* living room • *el comedor* dining room
el dormitorio bedroom • *el baño* bathroom • *¡Hola!* Hello! • *Yo me llamo . . .* • My name is . . .

YOU NEED

✔ **a pen**
✔ **crayons**
✔ **stickers showing a cooking pot, a TV, a pillow, a bottle of bubble bath**

1. Welcome to **Learn Spanish Anywhere.** With this activity kit you'll learn how to say things in Spanish, sing songs, and play games. Let's start right away with a game called "Home Planets." In this game, you get to pretend that you're from outer space!

2. Imagine you are an explorer from another planet discovering new worlds! Your mission is to report all you see to the Explorer-in-Chief, the Great Mirak. The Great Mirak speaks only Spanish, so you have to speak Spanish too. So, start the CD to learn your very first words in Spanish.

3. Pretend that each room is a new planet. Land your spaceship in the room, and start your report to the Great Mirak. First, say the Spanish name of the "room-planet" you're visiting. Then describe what it looks like. How big is it? Is it populated? If you see people on the planet, describe them too and explain what they do. For example, if they are on the "living-room planet," say: "They are adults and they watch TV."

4. Travel from "room-planet" to "room-planet," until you have explored the entire system of the home planets! Remember, the Great Mirak speaks only Spanish, so try to use as many Spanish words as possible in your report.

5. Whew! What a great trip you've just made. But wait! The game's not over. Now pick a partner. Pretend you are the Great Mirak and your partner is the explorer. He or she describes a "room-planet" without saying its name. You must guess which "room-planet" he or she is on. Can you name it in Spanish? Switch roles after you have guessed correctly.

6. Would you like to learn a Spanish rhyme about a special patio? It's called *El patio de mi casa* (My House's Patio). Quick, start on the CD!

7. Look at the house on the right-hand page. Do you know the name of each room in Spanish? If you already know how to read and write, write down the name of the room in Spanish. If you don't, ask an adult to help you. For each room, find the sticker with a thing you use in this room.

8. Draw your own room in the house on the bottom of the page and color it with crayons.

Home Planets

The Spanish House

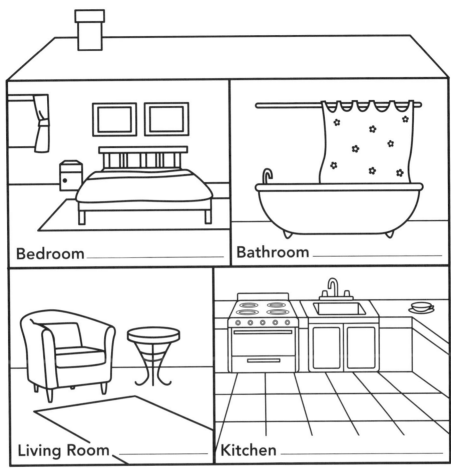

Bedroom _____

Bathroom _____

Living Room _____

Kitchen _____

Your Planet

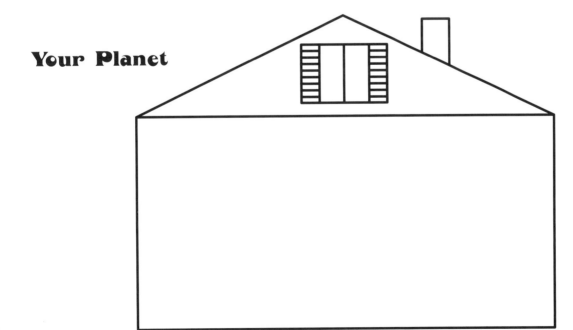

Interior Decorating

Time: 60 minutes

Vocabulary and Phrases: Furniture

los muebles furniture • *la cama* bed • *la mesa* table • *el escritorio* desk
la silla chair • *el sofá* sofa • *la lámpara* lamp • *la cómoda* chest of drawers

YOU NEED ·

✔ modeling clay
✔ stickers showing a bed, a table, a lamp, a chair
✔ a pen

· ·

1. Today we will furnish your entire house . . . with a little clay and a lot of imagination! Take out the modeling clay and pick a room. Can you say its name in Spanish? Good! Then start making pieces of furniture for this room with your clay. Be creative! Make the furniture you would like to see in this room. For example, if you picked the bedroom, make a round bed, a night table shaped like a frog, or a lamp shaped like a mushroom! There are no limits to your imagination.

2. When you're done with that room, count your score. Each piece you made is worth 10 points, but if you name it in Spanish, it's worth 20 points.

3. Now pick another room. Keep playing until you've furnished the entire house! What's your total score? To get a maximum number of points, start the CD and learn the Spanish names of some pieces of furniture.

4. To add a challenge, ask your parent or your teacher to pick a room and set a time limit.

Your parent or teacher will give you five minutes to make furniture for it. Count your points the same way; add a bonus 10 points if you name the room in Spanish!

5. If you have a partner, have him or her choose a room, and make clay furniture for it. As soon as one player is done, both must stop! Count your score as explained above (10 points for each piece, 20 points if you say its name in Spanish, and a bonus 10 points if you name the room in Spanish). Then switch roles so that now you pick the room and move on until you've covered the entire house. Tally your total score. The one with the higher number is the winner!

6. Find the answers to the questions on the right-hand page in the back of the book. Put the correct sticker next to each question. Can you write the name of the furniture in Spanish?

7. Imagine you are redecorating your bedroom. See the white roll of wallpaper? Draw the pattern you would like in your room.

Sticky Furniture

Where do you sleep?

Where do you eat?

What do you use to
have light at night?

Where do you sit
when you eat dinner?

Fancy Fun Wallpaper

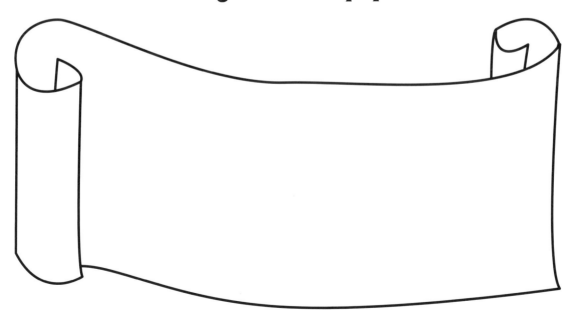

Time: 60 minutes

Vocabulary and Phrases: Weather Expressions

Está lloviendo. It's raining. • *Hace buen tiempo.* It's nice weather. • *Hace calor.* It's hot (weather).
Está nevando. It's snowing. • *Hace frío.* It's cold (weather).

YOU NEED ·

✔ a pen

· ·

1. Would you like to be a Detective or a Wizard? In this activity, you can be both! Be a Detective and find a hidden object, or be a Wizard and guide the detective on his or her search. Does that sound like fun?

2. You are Ace Inthehouse, a private detective. Your partner is the Weather Wizard. First, you, Ace, must pick a room where you will play. Give the Wizard the name of the room you picked in Spanish. Then the Wizard will go into that room alone. The Wizard will hide an object of his or her choice (like a toy). Then, he or she will call you back in the room.

3. Once you're back in the room, start looking for the hidden object. The Weather Wizard will give you clues with weather expressions. For example, if the Wizard says "It's hot," it means you are near the object. If the Wizard says "It's cold," you are moving away from it. To make the game more challenging, the Wizard will only speak Spanish! Start the CD now so you can learn some weather expressions in Spanish!

4. Ready? Here's the list of clues and what they mean.

Hace calor.	It's hot. (Ace is standing next to the object.)
Hace buen tiempo.	It's nice weather. (Ace is near the object.)
Está lloviendo.	It's raining. (Ace is walking toward the object.)
Hace frío.	It's cold. (Ace is walking away from the object.)
Está nevando.	It's snowing. (Ace is nowhere near the object.)

5. Go ahead and start playing! When you find what you think is the object, show it to your partner. Your partner will tell you if that's the right object or not. If it's not, keep playing! If it is, switch roles and pick another room of the house.

6. Did you like the game? Are you tired? Start the CD again to learn a little Spanish rhyme while you rest. It's called *Que llueva, que llueva* (Let It Rain, Let It Rain).

7. There's more fun on the right-hand page! See the drawings? If you use the object in the sun, draw a shining sun ☀ next to it. If you use the object in the rain, draw a rain cloud ☁.

8. Now, draw a snowman in the box. Don't forget to give it a hat and a nose!

or

   **Mr. Snowman**

Circle of Friends

Time: 60 minutes

Vocabulary and Phrases: Verbs

Canto. I sing. • *Salto.* I jump. • *Bailo.* I dance. • *Camino.* I walk.
Doy la vuelta. I turn. • *Me río.* I laugh. • *Lloro.* I cry. • *en el/la* in the

YOU NEED

✔ a pen
✔ crayons

1. In this fun activity you will mime different actions until there are too many to remember! Here's how to play. You and your friends sit in a circle on the floor. The first player will start by miming an action. The player can choose the action freely. For example, imagine you pick dancing. Stand up, say "I'm dancing," and take a few dance steps. A tango perhaps? (Just kidding.) Of course, you should say all this in Spanish.

2. The next player must copy the player before, and then add a second action, singing, for example. In this case he or she would say "I'm dancing," mime dancing, then say "I'm singing," and sing a few notes. The next player will repeat those two actions and add another. And so on with each player.

3. Keep going from player to player around the circle until someone makes a mistake, such as forgetting an action or mixing up the right sequence of actions. Then start a new game. It's easy, isn't it? And don't forget the challenge of the game: you must speak as much Spanish as possible. Start the CD to learn the words you'll need.

4. More fun with Spanish actions? Why not play a game of "Simon Says" using the words you've just learned? To learn how to play that game, go to the next activity, "Simon Says," and replace the words suggested there with the ones you've just learned.

5. Which animal jumps? Which one walks? In the boxes on the right-hand page, draw one animal that jumps, and one that walks.

6. Now take your crayons and color all the animals in the zoo. Do you remember what those Spanish words mean? Why don't you write the English next to them?

¡Salto! (I Jump!)   *¡Camino!* (I Walk!)

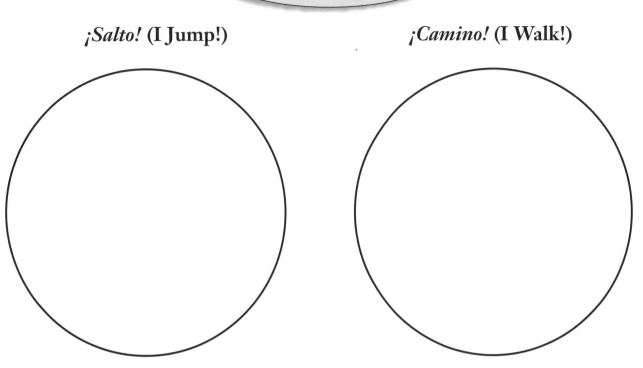

Zoo Party!

Salta

Canta

Baila

Camina

Simon Says

Time: 30 minutes

Vocabulary and Phrases: The Body
la cabeza head • *el brazo* arm • *la mano* hand • *la pierna* leg • *el pie* foot
la cara face • *el cuerpo* body • *Simón dice* . . . Simon says . . .

YOU NEED ·

✔ a pen
✔ stickers showing an arm, a foot, a hand

· ·

1. Here's an activity that will make you use your entire body. In this version of "Simon Says," you will give orders in Spanish. Will your partner obey you? Read on!

2. The game is easy. Give an order to your partner. If you say the Spanish phrase for "Simon says . . . ," *Simón dice*, before you give the order, your partner must obey it. If you don't say it, he or she must not move! Another thing: all your orders must ask your partner to do something with a part of the body, such as "wave your hand" or "turn your head."

3. Since this is a Spanish game, you must say "*Simón dice* . . ." and the parts of the body in Spanish. So quick, Simon says . . . start the CD now to learn how.

4. Remember: if your partner makes a mistake, he or she is out. If you have several partners, play until there's only one player left. This player then becomes the one to give orders. If you have only one partner, play until he or she makes a mistake, then switch roles. Don't forget to use as many Spanish words as you can.

5. For variation, give orders using the Spanish verbs you learned in the activity called "Circle of Friends." For example: "Simon says: I dance," or "I jump!" How do you say that in Spanish?*

6. Do you want to sing *Llega la mañana* (The Morning Is Here), a Spanish song about the daily morning routine of a child? Start the CD again.

7. Uh-oh . . . There's a creature on the right-hand page and it's missing some body parts! Complete its body by adding the stickers with the missing parts.

8. Now that the creature is complete, connect its body parts so they can work. To do that, match each name in the left column with the part it is attached to in the right column. (For example, the neck is attached to the head.) When you're done, draw the body part next to its name. Can you name some of them in Spanish?

* I dance = *Bailo;* I jump = *Salto*

The Creature

Connect the Creature

This is attached to...   **what?**

nose   leg

hand   face

fingers   head

toes   hand

foot   arm

neck   foot

Dice Man

Time: 45 minutes

Vocabulary and Phrases: Numbers

uno one • *dos* two • *tres* three • *cuatro* four • *cinco* five • *seis* six
siete seven • *ocho* eight • *nueve* nine • *diez* ten • *once* eleven • *doce* twelve

YOU NEED

✔ 2 dice
✔ 2 pens
✔ 2 pieces of paper

✔ a calculator
✔ stickers with a die showing 2, a die showing 4

1. Here's a game where you roll the dice to draw a Dice Man! Choose a partner. You each need a pen and a piece of paper. You also need two dice. The point of the game is to draw the figure of a man (the Dice Man) before your partner. The trick is that you must roll the dice to know which part of the Dice Man you can draw!

2. Before you begin, each player must roll the dice once. The player with the higher number starts the game. Then that player rolls the dice again to start the game. The sum of the two dice determines what to draw. Say the sum in Spanish to get another turn! (You only get to draw again once. The next turn is your partner's, even if you said the sum in Spanish.) So start the CD to learn how to count in Spanish!

3. Go ahead: roll the dice! If you get a . . .
    two (2): draw the head
    three (3): don't draw, lose your turn
    four (4): don't draw, lose your turn
    five (5): draw a hand (left or right)
    six (6): draw a leg (left or right)
    seven (7): don't draw, lose your turn
    eight (8): draw a foot (left or right)

   nine (9): don't draw, lose your turn
   ten (10): draw an arm (left or right)
   eleven (11): don't draw, lose your turn
   twelve (12): draw the body

4. If you get a sum for a body part you've already drawn, you must also pass your turn, unless you can name that part of the body in Spanish. In that case, you get to roll the dice one extra time. (To remember how to say the parts of the body, see the activity called "Simon Says . . .") Are you ready? Great! Start rolling and drawing!

5. Aren't numbers fun? Look on the right-hand page. Use a calculator to solve each math problem. Write down the result, then turn the calculator upside down and . . . see a secret word appear on the screen!

6. Now break the calculator code! Write the letter each number spells when read upside down on the screen. Can you make up more words with these topsy-turvy numbers?

7. Finally, look at the dice and find the two stickers with the corresponding answers.

Words by Numbers

$$600 + 37 =$$

$$7000 + 334 =$$

$$210 + 7 =$$

$$3700 + 4 =$$

Secret Word . . .[1]

_____

_____

_____

_____

Topsy-Turvy Calculator Code . . .[2]

$0 =$ $1 =$ $2 =$ $3 =$ $4 =$

$5 =$ $6 =$ $7 =$ $8 =$

  = [3]

  =

Time: 60 minutes

Vocabulary and Phrases: Facial Features

la máscara mask • *los ojos* eyes • *la nariz* nose • *la boca* mouth
las orejas ears • *el cabello* hair • *pequeño(a)* small • *redondo(a)* round

YOU NEED ·

✔ three or four white paper plates
✔ glue
✔ scissors

✔ materials to create and decorate masks, such as crayons, paints, aluminum foil, fabric swatches, colored strings, ribbons, wool, or felt

· ·

1. In "The Mask," you're going to make, well, a mask! First, gather all the materials you need: a couple of white paper plates, scissors (be careful with these; ask an adult for permission and help), colored crayons and/or paint, and a little glue (you'll need an adult's permission and help for this as well).

2. After that, search for pieces of string, colored paper, fabric swatches, wool, aluminum foil, or pipe cleaners (remember to get an adult's permission and help). You can put anything you think may be interesting on your mask.

3. All finished? Good. Now sit at the table and spread all this before you. But before you start making your mask, start the CD to learn all about the Spanish face!

4. Now you're ready to make your mask. Are you going to make an animal? A superhero? A cartoon character? You decide! Take a paper plate and cut out two holes for the eyes and one hole for the nose. Do you remember what these features are called in Spanish? Next, draw, paint, or cut out the mouth, and add the ears. To do

these, you can glue pieces of paper or fabric. Finally, add the hair. Draw it, or glue pieces of string, aluminum foil, felt, or anything you see fit! Use your imagination!

5. As you go along, name each part of the face you are doing in Spanish. You can also say whether each is small or round in Spanish, can't you? When you're done, ask an adult to help you punch two little holes on both sides of the mask and tie a string through each. Then put on your mask and play!

6. There's a face looking at you on the right-hand page. But wait! It's missing something! Can you find the stickers that complete the face? Do you remember what these are called in Spanish? These four Spanish words are hidden in the little puzzle. Look carefully in every direction!

7. Do you have two noses and one ear? Or one nose and two ears? Put a checkmark (✔) in the box that corresponds to the number of facial features you have. To make things more challenging, we've written the names in Spanish! After that, draw each part next to its name.

Look at Me!

Face Puzzle

```
S   Y   Z   I   R   A   N
O   R   E   J   A   S   A
J   H   A   C   O   B   R
O   K   B   Y   X   A   Z
```

One or Two?

	one	two
los ojos	❏	❏
la boca	❏	❏
las orejas	❏	❏
la nariz	❏	❏

Find the Rainbow

Time: 45 minutes

Vocabulary and Phrases: Colors

el color color • *rojo* red • *azul* blue • *negro* black
blanco white • *amarillo* yellow • *verde* green

YOU NEED ·

  ✔ paper
  ✔ crayons or colored pencils

· ·

1. Play "Find the Rainbow," and color your day! Take out your crayons or colored pencils. You'll need red, blue, black, white, yellow, and green. Don't worry if you don't have every color. You'll also need some sheets of paper. How will you "Find the Rainbow?" Before we explain, start the CD to learn how to say the colors in Spanish.

2. Okay, now you're ready. We'll play this game in the house. Start the game in your bedroom. Can you name that room in Spanish? Great! Now pick one of these colors:

  red *(rojo)*   blue *(azul)*
  white *(blanco)* yellow *(amarillo)*
  green *(verde)*   black *(negro)*

Say its name in Spanish, or write it on top of a sheet of paper. Then take a crayon in that color. If you don't have the exact color, take a crayon that has a similar tint (like yellow for white).

3. Now let's play! To "Find the Rainbow," you must look all around the house for 10 things in the color you picked. Each time you see something that color, draw it and/or write down its name. Once you have 10 things on your paper, go back to your room and pick another color, another crayon, and another piece of paper. Look for 10 things in that new color. Keep playing until you've gone through the entire list of colors. At the end, you'll have a rainbow . . . of papers!

4. Now play with a partner: one of you picks a color, then you both go look for things in that color. As soon as one player has ten things on his or her paper, the other must stop looking. Count 10 points for each drawing, 20 points for each written name, plus an extra 20 points if you name the color in Spanish! The player with the higher score picks another color. Keep playing until you've gone through the entire list of colors. Tally your scores. The player with the higher score wins the title of "Supreme Rainbow Seeker."

5. There's more colorful fun on the right-hand page. First, draw a rainbow in the box. Do you know the color of each of the things below the rainbow? Can you write or say the Spanish name of the color?

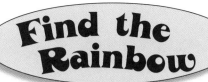

My Rainbow

Colors!

The grass is . . .

The sky is . . .

The sun is . . .

A fire truck is . . .

The snow is . . .

Licorice is . . .

Captain Cook

Time: 30 minutes

Vocabulary and Phrases: Fruits

la manzana apple • *la pera* pear • *el plátano* banana • *la fresa* strawberry • *el melocotón* peach
la cereza cherry • *las uvas* grapes • *la ensalada de frutas* fruit salad

YOU NEED

For the fruit salad:
- ✔ at least five of these fruits: banana, apple, pear, peach, nectarine, plum, kiwi, apricot, grapes, cherries, pineapple chunks, strawberries
- ✔ a big bowl
- ✔ ¼ cup of water or fruit juice (orange or pineapple)

- ✔ 4 tablespoons of granulated sugar
- ✔ a big spoon
- ✔ a knife

For the game:
- ✔ a pen
- ✔ stickers with a banana, an apple, grapes

1. In this activity, you are "Captain Cook," the great TV chef. Today, in your show "Captain Cook Cooks," you are going to explain how to make a great fruit salad.

2. Go into the kitchen and get ready to record your show. First, with the help of an adult (every big chef has an assistant), put everything you need on the table in front of you. Ready? Wait a second! Like many famous chefs, you are Spanish. So quick, start the CD to learn the Spanish names of some fruits!

3. Now start making your salad. Remember to use as much Spanish as possible when explaining each step of the recipe. Ready? Camera! Action! Carefully wash all the fruits you have. Peel the fruits that have a skin you can't eat (like the banana, the orange, the kiwi . . .). Then ask an adult assistant to cut each fruit into bite-size cubes. Put the cubes in the bowl.

4. Mix the water or the fruit juice with the sugar, and pour the mixture over the fruits in the bowl. Stir with a big spoon. Taste. Add some sugar and/or water (or juice) if needed.

5. Now your bowl is full of colorful fruits. Present it to the public, and tell them what's in it. Can you name some of the fruits in Spanish? And can you say what color they are, too?

6. Now look at the ingredients on the right-hand page. Which ones are used to make a cake? Cross out those that don't go in a cake, and circle the ones that do.

7. One more thing: see the empty bowl? Fill it with three stickers representing fruits. Can you say and/or write their Spanish names? And why don't you draw a few more fruits yourself?

Bake a Cake!

   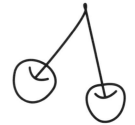

Full of Fruits!

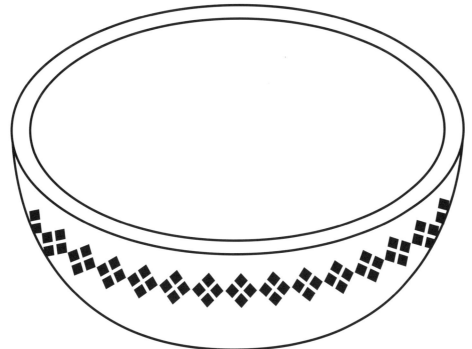

Raiders of the House

Time: 60 minutes

Vocabulary and Phrases: Objects

el tesoro treasure • *el jabón* soap • *el cepillo de dientes* toothbrush • *los cereales* cereals
el tazón bowl • *el control remoto* remote control • *el peluche* plush toy • *el libro* book • *la pelota* ball

YOU NEED ·

✔ a pen

· ·

1. In "Raiders of the House," you search the house to find a treasure. The first player to find it is the best "Raider of the House"! Doesn't that sound like fun? It is! So quick, before you start raiding, start the CD to learn what to call the things you'll look for in Spanish.

2. Here's the list of things you must find:
    soap (*el jabón*)
    a toothbrush (*el cepillo de dientes*)
    cereals (*los cereales*)
    a bowl (*el tazón*)
    remote control (*el control remoto*)
    a book (*el libro*)
    a plush toy (*el peluche*)
    a ball (*la pelota*)

3. Ready? You and your partner must race around the house to find these things. The game stops when one player has collected everything. But wait! There's one more challenge: If you can name the object you found in Spanish, you get 20 points. If you can't, you get no points at all!

Name the room where you found it in Spanish, too, and you get an extra 10 points. Finally, say the color of the treasure in Spanish, and add 5 points! Total your points. See, even if you haven't found everything, you can still win! You need only speak Spanish to be the supreme "Raider of the House."

4. For variation, add more objects to your list (check out the activity called "Forget-Me-Not" for another list of objects in Spanish). You can choose a theme, like furniture or fruits (look at the activities called "Interior Decorating" and "Captain Cook" to add some Spanish words to your list).

5. Are you tired of running around the house? Sit down and look at all those lines on the right-hand page. Follow each one to find each raider's treasure. That done, why don't you draw *your* treasure, your absolute favorite thing, in the box?

Treasure Mix

My Treasure

Let's Find a Disguise!

Time: 60 minutes

Vocabulary and Phrases: Clothes

la princesa princess • *el pirata* pirate • *el vestido* dress • *el pantalón* pants
la camisa shirt • *la chaqueta* jacket • *la falda* skirt • *el sombrero* hat
largo, larga long • *corto, corta* short • *Yo soy . . .* I am . . .

YOU NEED ·

✔ **different pieces of clothing to choose from: dresses, pants, shirts, vests, skirts, hats . . .**
✔ **aluminum foil (optional)**
✔ **a big brown bag (optional)**
✔ **paints or crayons**
✔ **stickers showing a crown, a firefighter helmet, a plumed hat**

· ·

1. Look in the mirror. What do you see? Yourself, of course. But can you imagine what you would look like if you were a pirate or a princess? Here's how you find out! First, you need to pick a disguise. Will you be a pirate or a princess? Something else? Choose the disguise you want. Then go to your bedroom with a partner and ask him or her to help you put a costume together.

2. Since you are taking on a new identity, why don't you use your new language as well? Start the CD to hear the Spanish names of clothes.

3. Are you ready? Use Spanish words to ask your partner to give you the clothes you need for your costume. Switch turns once your costume is finished.

4. You can complete your costume with aluminum foil or a large paper bag. Take some foil and shape it into a crown, or a sword. If you

need to wear something special (like an astronaut suit, or a robot top) use a large paper bag. Cut a hole big enough for your head on top, and cut a hole on each side for your arms. Then take your paints or crayons to decorate your outfit.

5. If you want to complete your costume with a mask, you can make one yourself with a paper plate. To learn how, look at the activity called "The Mask."

6. Look! It's Halloween on the right-hand page! See the kids in costume? One is a firefighter, one is a king, the other a great duchess. Only they are each missing something: a hat! Put the sticker with the right hat on each of their heads. When you're done, color the costume of the Harlequin.

Hat Tricks

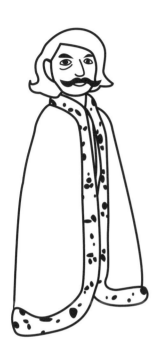  

Harlequin

Pick a Pet

Time: 30 minutes

Vocabulary and Phrases: Pets

el gato cat • *el perro* dog • *el pájaro* bird • *el pez* fish • *el conejo* rabbit
el hámster hamster • *la tortuga* turtle • *la mascota* pet

YOU NEED

✔ a pen
✔ stickers showing a doghouse, a birdcage, a fishbowl

1. Are pets important in your life? Well, they are important in this game where you "Pick a Pet" and mime it. Your partner must guess the pet you are miming and give his or her answer in Spanish. So start the CD to learn what your favorite pets are called in Spanish.

2. Ready? Pick, and mime! If your partner guesses correctly, switch turns. If not, keep miming! Remember: you must answer in Spanish.

3. When you're done playing, start the CD again to hear some animal sounds in the Spanish song called *La cancíon de los pollitos* (The Baby Chick Song).

4. Pets are good company, so let's stay with them on the right-hand page. Find the sticker that shows where each animal lives and put it next to it. Can you say and/or write the Spanish name of each animal? Wonderful!

5. Now, read or say the name of each animal. Is it a pet or a wild animal? If it's a pet, draw a little house next to it. If it's a wild animal, draw a tree.

Pick a Pet

Pet Place

Pet or Wild?

tiger

puppy

gorilla

cat

Time: 60 minutes

Vocabulary and Phrases: Birthday Things

el cumpleaños birthday • *la tarjeta* card • *la sorpresa* sorpresa • *el regalo* gift
el pastel cake • *la vela* candle • *feliz* happy • *¡Feliz cumpleaños!* Happy birthday!
Gracias. Thank you. • *Tengo . . . años.* I am . . . years old.

YOU NEED

✔ a card-size piece of white cardboard, or stiff drawing paper
✔ several old magazines
✔ crayons or paints
✔ scissors
✔ glue
✔ a sticker with 4 candles; stickers reading *Feliz* and *cumpleaños*

1. Is someone you love having a birthday soon? Perhaps *you* are. In this activity, you'll make a birthday card with a Spanish twist.

2. Your Spanish birthday card is a collage of different things that have to do with birthdays. Before you start, start the CD to learn what these things are.

3. Ready? Good! Then let's prepare your material. You need a card-size piece of white cardboard, or stiff drawing paper. You also need various old magazines, crayons or paints, glue, and scissors. Remember: you must ask an adult for permission to use the glue and the scissors.

4. Now look in the magazines for pictures of things you use when you celebrate a birthday. Ask an adult to help you cut out pictures of a card, a cake, presents, birthday candles, flowers, and chocolates. Arrange them on your blank card. Move them around to see what looks best. Ask an adult to help you glue these pictures in place. Wait for the card to dry.

5. Once the card is dry, take your crayons or paints and write "Happy Birthday" in Spanish on your card. You can also write the Spanish names of some of the things pictured on your card.

6. Of course a birthday is not a birthday without the special birthday song. Start the CD to sing *Feliz cumpleaños*—that's "Happy Birthday" in Spanish.

7. There's more celebration on the right-hand page. Can you find the stickers that complete the birthday cake? You need candles and the Spanish words for "happy birthday". When you're done, color the cake.

Make a Cake

Forget-Me-Not

Time: 30 minutes

Vocabulary and Phrases: More Objects

la galleta cookie • *el reloj* watch • *la fotografía* photograph
la cinta cassette tape • *la pluma* pen • *el cepillo* hairbrush • *el dado* die

YOU NEED ·

✔ a tray
✔ a towel
✔ a pen
✔ stickers with the words *el reloj, el dado, la cinta, la pluma, la fotografía*

· ·

1. Play "Forget-Me-Not" and improve your memory! In this game, your partner will have to remember the objects you put on a tray. So pick a partner, then get a tray and a towel. But first start the CD to learn the Spanish words that will earn you more points.

2. Ready? Put the following objects on the tray: cookie(s), hairbrush(es), watch(es), pen(s), photograph(s), die (dice), and cassette tape(s). One object can appear more than once. For example, you can put two dice or three pens on the tray. Show the tray to your partner and count to 10. Can you do that in Spanish? (Go back to the activity called "Dice Man" for help.) Then cover the tray with the towel and ask your partner what was on it.

3. Count 10 points for each object your partner remembers correctly and 20 points if he or she names it in Spanish. Here's a super Spanish bonus: count 5 points each time your partner gives the correct number in Spanish of a particular object (like *tres* cookies), and 5 points each

time he or she tells the color in Spanish of an object (like a *pluma roja* for a red pen).

4. Switch turns. Your partner keeps the same objects on the tray, but adds variation. For example, he or she may put two blue pens instead of one red pen on the tray. Or one die instead of two. Play as described. At the end of your turn, compare your scores. Who wins? The one with the highest score of course!

5. If you want to keep on playing, change the objects on the tray. Use toothbrush(es), hat(s), remote control(s), birthday card(s), apple(s), plush toy(s), and bowl(s). Look throughout this book to remember what they're called in Spanish.

6. For each thing on the right-hand page, find the sticker with its corresponding Spanish name and put it next to the object. That done, draw the face of the watch you would love to have. Don't forget to put in the numbers! Can you say them in Spanish?

Forget-Me-Not

Call Me!

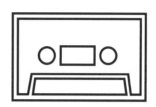

Time to Watch

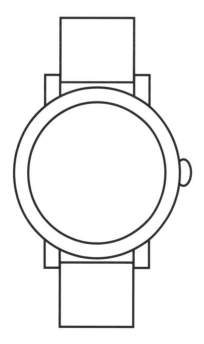

Time: 45 minutes

Vocabulary and Phrases: Animals That Like Water

el tiburón shark • *la ballena* whale • *el delfín* dolphin • *el cocodrilo* crocodile
el pato duck • *el sapo* frog • *agresivo* mean • *agradable* nice

YOU NEED ·

✔ a pen
✔ stickers showing a crocodile, a duck, a shark, a whale, a dolphin

· ·

1. Pretend you are an animal as you play "Water Beast." Since this is a game about water animals, why not go play in the bathroom? Do you remember how to say "bathroom" in Spanish? Go there with your partner. To play, you need to know the Spanish names of some animals that like water, so start the CD.

2. Pick one of these animals: fish, turtle, crocodile, dolphin, duck, whale, frog, or shark. Then say: "If I were a Water Beast, I would . . ." and describe two things you would do, such as what you would eat, or where you would live. Your partner must guess which animal you are talking about and give his or her answer in Spanish. As an extra clue, add whether this animal is mean or nice in Spanish.

3. If your partner guesses correctly, switch turns. If not, add another description, and another, and another . . . until your partner guesses correctly. Remember to use the Spanish names of these animals!

4. You'll find more "Water Beasts" on the right-hand page. See the written names? Find the sticker that shows each animal and put it next to its name. Can you also say and/or write its Spanish name?

5. Now find the five Spanish names in the puzzle. Don't forget to look in every direction, even upside down!

See Me Swim!

crocodile   shark   whale

duck   dolphin

Find Us!

pez								delfín
	X	T	O	B	Z	E	P	N
	P	I	S	R	R	A	C	P
ballena	G	B	A	L	L	E	N	A	tiburón
	J	U	Q	A	P	E	O	T
pato	R	R	K	V	U	Y	A	O
	Q	O	R	K	D	E	A	H
	B	N	I	F	L	E	D	I

Days of the Week

Time: 45 minutes

Vocabulary and Phrases: The Seven Days of the Week

lunes Monday • *martes* Tuesday • *miércoles* Wednesday • *jueves* Thursday • *viernes* Friday
sábado Saturday • *domingo* Sunday • *el fin de semana* weekend • *el día* day • *la semana* week

YOU NEED ·

✔ paper
✔ a pen
✔ an old TV listing (optional)
✔ a new TV listing (optional)
✔ scissors and glue (optional)

· ·

1. Do you use a TV listing to decide what you're going to watch on TV? Of course you do. In "Days of the Week," you make your own TV listing!

2. To start, you need a Spanish weekly calendar. So start the CD to learn how to say the days of the week in Spanish.

3. Write the seven days of the week in Spanish on a piece of paper (see the right-hand page for a model). For each day, invent the name of a TV show you'd like to watch. Say or write that name down. If you don't want to make up new shows, use the names of the TV shows you usually watch. You can also draw a clock showing the time at which each show is playing.

4. If you prefer, use an old TV listing and cut out the names and/or the illustrations of the TV shows you love. Glue them in your calendar under the day you watch that show. Be careful: ask an adult for permission and help before you use scissors and glue.

5. Now take this week's TV listing. With the help of an adult, decide which show you will watch each day and write its name and the time it's on in your calendar. When you're done, you can post your TV program in your bedroom.

6. Start the CD again to learn *Tilingo, tilingo,* a Spanish rhyme about a frog's wedding.

7. Use the calendar on the right-hand page to note the weather this week. You can draw the weather (like a sunshine), or write it down. Can you say the weather in Spanish? See "Ace Inthehouse, Detective" to help you remember how. Why not note it in Spanish?

8. For each day, you can add an activity you did or any other important information. Was it somebody's birthday? Did you get some new clothes? Try to use as much Spanish as possible!

Days of the Week

Dear Daily Diary

lunes	
martes	
miércoles	
jueves	
viernes	
sábado	
domingo	

Appendixes

Songs and Rhymes

EL PATIO DE MI CASA

El patio de mi casa
Es particular
Cuando llueve se moja
Como los demás.
Agáchate y vuélvete a agachar
Que los agachaditos
Sí saben bailar.
H, I, J, K, L, M, N, O
Que si tú no me quieres
Otro amante me querrá.
H, I, ,J, K, L, M, N, O
Que si tú no me quieres
Otro amante tendré yo.

QUE LLUEVA, QUE LLUEVA

Que llueva, que llueva
La vieja está en la cueva
Los pajaritos cantan,
Las nubes se levantan
Que sí, que no
¡Que caiga un chaparrón!

MY HOUSE'S PATIO

My house has a
private yard,
But it gets wet when it rains
Like any other patio.
Bend your body, bend it again,
Those who bend their bodies
Know how to dance.
H, I, J, K, L, M, N, O
If you do not love me
Someone else will love me back
H, I, J, K, L, M, N, O
If you do not love me
I'll find someone else.

LET IT RAIN, LET IT RAIN

Let it rain, let it rain
The old lady's in the cave
The birds are singing,
The clouds have risen.
Oh yes, oh, no!
I wish it would pour today!

LLEGA LA MAÑANA

Llega la mañana
Hay que levantarse,
Lavarse la cara
Y después peinarse.
Esto no me gusta,
Lo tengo enredado
Mi cabello se queja
Lo han lastimado. La, la, lalalala . . .
La, la, lalalala . . .
Me voy a la escuela
Tocan la campana
Por entrar corriendo
Quedé castigada
Por fin el recreo,
No traje cordel,
Tampoco pelota
¡Qué vamos a hacer!
La, la, lalalala . . .

LA CANCIÓN DE LOS POLLITOS

Los pollitos dicen pío, pío, pío
Cuando tienen hambre,
Cuando tienen frío.
La gallina busca el maíz y el trigo
Les da la comida
Y les presta abrigo.
Bajo sus dos alas, acurrucaditos
Hasta el otro día
Duermen los pollitos.

THE MORNING IS HERE

The morning is here
I have to get up,
Wash my face
And comb my hair.
I don't like this,
My hair is tangled up,
My hair complains
It's been hurt. La, la, lalalala
La, la, lalalala . . .
I go to school
I hear the bell ring
I get punished
because I enter running.
At last comes recess,
I forgot the rope,
I forgot the ball,
What can we do!
La, la, lalalala . . .

THE BABY CHICK SONG

The baby chicks cry pio, pio, pio
When they get hungry
When they get cold
The mother hen looks for corn and wheat,
Then gives them food
And gives them shelter
Under her two wings, snuggled in
Until the next day
the chicks sleep.

FELIZ CUMPLEAÑOS

Feliz cumpleaños,
Feliz cumpleaños a ti,
Feliz cumpleaños querido Juan
Feliz cumpleaños a ti.

TILINGO, TILINGO

Tilingo, tilingo
Mañana es domingo
Se casa la rana
Con Juan Domingo
¿Quién es la madrina?
Juana Catalina.
¿Quién es el padrino?
Pepe Barrigón.
Quien hable primero
Se traga el tapón.
Yo no me lo trago
Porque tengo las llaves de San Simón.

HAPPY BIRTHDAY

Happy birthday,
Happy birthday to you,
Happy birthday dear [your name here]
Happy birthday to you!

DING-DONG, DING-DONG

Ding-dong, ding-dong
Tomorrow is Sunday
The frog is getting married
With Juan Domingo.
Who is the bridesmaid?
Juana Catalina.
Who is the best man?
Pepe Big Belly.
Whoever speaks first
Will eat the cork.
I cannot eat it
Because I am holding the keys of
Saint Simon.

Glossary

Notes
- All Spanish nouns and adjectives have a gender. They are either masculine or feminine. The article preceding the noun indicates the gender of the noun: *el* and *un* (the, a) are masculine articles, *la* and *una* are feminine articles. The plural articles are *los/las* and *unos/unas*.
- To form the plural of most nouns, simply add a final "s" to the noun. Some nouns have an irregular plural. In this glossary, irregular plurals are indicated in parentheses (pl.) after the singular noun.
- All adjectives agree in gender and number with the noun they modify. In this glossary, the feminine form of an adjective is indicated in parentheses (f.) after its masculine form.
- All words marked with an asterisk (*) are extended vocabulary not introduced in the program.

Spanish–English

A
agradable	nice
agresivo (f. *agresiva*)	mean
amarillo (f. *amorilla*)	yellow
el animal	animal

♦ AQUATIC ANIMALS ♦	
la ballena	whale
*el cangrejo**	crab
*el cisne**	swan
el cocodrilo	crocodile
el delfín	dolphin
*la foca**	seal
*la nutria**	otter
el pato	duck
*el pinguino**	penguin
el sapo	frog
el tiburón	shark

*el año**	year

♦ THE YEAR ♦	
*el año**	year
el día	day
la hora	hour
*el mes**	month
la semana	week

azul	blue

B
bailar	dance
Bailo.	I dance.
la ballena	whale
el banano	banana
el baño	bathroom
blanco (f. *blanca*)	white
el brazo	arm
buen tiempo	nice, pretty weather
buena suerte	good luck

C
el cabello	hair
la cabeza	head
la cama	bed
caminar	to walk
Camino.	I walk.
la camisa	shirt
cantar	to sing
la cara	face

♦ THE FACE ♦	
la barbilla	chin
la boca	mouth
el cabello	hair
las cejas	eyebrows
*los dientes**	teeth
los labios	lips
*la mejilla**	cheek
la nariz	nose
los ojos	eyes
la oreja	ear

la casa	house

♦ AT HOME ♦	
*el ático**	attic
el baño	bathroom
la cocina	kitchen
el comedor	dining room
el dormitorio	bedroom
*el garaje**	garage
*el pasillo**	hall
*la puerta**	door
*el ropero**	closet
la sala	living room
*el sótano**	basement

cepillo	brush (hair)
cepillo de dientes	toothbrush
los cereales	cereals
la cereza	cherry
cinco	five
la chaqueta	jacket

el chocolate	chocolate
la cinta	tape
el cocodrilo	crocodile
la cocina	kitchen
el color	color
los colores	colors

♦ COLORS ♦	
amarillo(a)	yellow
anaranjado(a)	orange
azul	blue
blanco(a)	white
*marrón**	brown
morado(a)	purple
negro(a)	black
rojo(a)	red
*rosado(a)**	pink
verde	green
*violeta**	purple

el comedor	dining room
la cómoda	chest of drawers
el conejo	rabbit
el control remoto	remote control
corto (f. *corta*)	short
cuatro	four
el cuerpo	body

♦ THE BODY ♦	
el brazo	arm
la cabeza	head
*el codo**	elbow
la espalda	back
*el estómago**	stomach
la mano	hand
el pie	foot
la pierna	leg
el vientre	belly

D
el dado	dice
el delfín	dolphin
el día	day
los días de la semana	days of the week
dice	he/she says
diez	ten
doce	twelve
domingo	Sunday
el dormitorio	bedroom
dos	two

DAYS OF THE WEEK

lunes	Monday
martes	Tuesday
miércoles	Wednesday
jueves	Thursday
viernes	Friday
sábado	Saturday
domingo	Sunday

E

en el/la . . .	in the. . .
la ensalada de frutas	fruit salad
el escritorio	desk
Está lloviendo.	It's raining.
Está nevando.	It's snowing.

EXPRESSIONS

¡Adiós!	Goodbye!
¡Feliz cumpleaños!	Happy birthday!
¡Feliz año nuevo!*	Happy New Year!
¡Gracias.	Thank you.
¡Hasta la vista!	See you soon!
¡Hola!	Hello!

F

la falda	skirt
¡Feliz cumpleaños!	Happy birthday!
el fin de semana	weekend
la flor	flower
la fresa	strawberry
frío (f. fria)	cold
las frutas	fruits

FRUITS

el albaricoque*	apricot
la cereza	cherry
la ciruela*	plum
la fresa	strawberry
el limón*	lemon
el mango*	mango
la manzana	apple
el melocotón	peach
la naranja	orange
la pera	pear
la piña*	pineapple
el plátano	banana

G

la galleta	cookie
el gato	cat
Gracias.	Thank you.

H

hacer	to do

Hace buen tiempo.	It's nice (weather).
Hace mal tiempo.	It's bad (weather).
Hace calor.	It's hot (weather).
Hace frío.	It's cold (weather).
el hámster	hamster
¡Hola!	Hello!

J

el jabón	soap

L

la lámpara	lamp
largo (f. larga)	long
el libro	book
lunes	Monday
llorar	to cry
Llueve.	It's raining.
la lluvia	rain

M

la mano	hand
martes	Tuesday
la máscara	mask
la mascota	pet

PETS

el cachorro	puppy
el cochinillo de Indias*	guinea pig
el conejo	rabbit
la culebra	snake
el gato	cat
el gatito*	kitten
el hámster	hamster
el pájaro	bird
el perro	dog
la pez	fish
el ratón*	mouse
el serpiente*	snake

la manzana	apple
el melocotón	peach
la mesa	table
Me llamo . . .	My name is . . .
miércoles	Wednesday
los muebles	furniture

FURNITURE

el armario*	wardrobe
la cama	bed
la cómoda	chest of drawers
el estante*	shelf
la lámpara	lamp
el librero*	bookcase
la mesa	table
la mesa de noche*	bedside table
la poltrona*	armchair
la silla	chair
el sofá	sofa

N

la nariz	nose
negro (f. negra)	black
nevar	to snow
Está nevando.	It's snowing.
la nieve	snow
no	no
el número	number

NUMBERS

uno	one
dos	two
tres	three
cuatro	four
cinco	five
seis	six
siete	seven
ocho	eight
nueve	nine
diez	ten
once	eleven
doce	twelve
veinte*	twenty
cincuenta*	fifty
cien*	one hundred
mil*	one thousand
un millón*	one million

nueve	nine

O

ocho	eight
los ojos	eyes
once	eleven
la oreja	ear

P

el pájaro	bird
el pantalón	pants
el pastel	cake
el pato	duck
el peluche	plush toy
pequeño (f. pequeña)	small
la pera	pear
el perro	dog
el pez	fish
el pie	foot
la pierna	leg
el pirata	pirate
la pluma	pen
la princesa	princess

R

reír (se)	to laugh
Me río.	I'm laughing.
el regalo	present
redondo (f. redonda)	round
rojo (f. roja)	red
el reloj	watch
la ropa	clothes

✦ ✦ ✦ CLOTHES ✦ ✦ ✦

el abrigo*	coat
las botas*	boots
la camisa	shirt
la camiseta*	T-shirt
la chaqueta	jacket
la falda	skirt
las medias*	socks
el pantalón	pants
el sombrero*	hat
el suéter	sweater
los vaqueros/ maones*	jeans
el vestido	dress
los zapatos	shoes

S

el sábado	Saturday
la sala	living room
saltar	to jump
Yo salto.	I jump.
el sapo	frog
seis	six
la semana	week
ser	to be
sí	yes
siete	seven
la silla	chair
Simón dice . . .	Simon says . . .
el sofá	sofa
el sombrero	hat
la sorpresa	surprise
soy	I am

T

la tarjeta	card
el tazón	bowl
tener	to have
Tengo . . . años.	I am . . . years old.
el tesoro	treasure
el tiempo	weather

✦ ✦ ✦ WEATHER ✦ ✦ ✦

Está helado.	It's freezing.
Está lloviendo.	It's raining.
Está nevando.	It's snowing.
Hace buen tiempo.	It's nice weather.
Hace calor.	It's hot.
la lluvia	rain
la nieve	snow
el relámpago	lightning
el tiempo	weather
el trueno*	thunder

la tortuga	turtle
tres	three

U

uno (f. una)	one
las uvas	grapes

V

la vela	candle
verde	green
viernes	Friday

Y

yo	I
Yo soy	I am

English–Spanish

A

animal	el animal
apple	la manzana
arm	el brazo

✦ AQUATIC ANIMALS ✦

crocodile	el cocodrilo
dolphin	el delfín
duck	el pato
frog	el sapo
otter	la nutria*
penguin	el pinguino*
seal	la foca*
shark	el tiburón
swan	el cisne*
whale	la ballena

B

banana	el plátano/el banano
bathroom	el baño
to be	ser
I am . . .	Yo soy . . .
I am . . . years old.	Tengo . . . años.
bed	la cama
bedroom	el dormitorio
bird	el pájaro (pl. los pájaros)

✦ ✦ ✦ THE BODY ✦ ✦ ✦

arm	el brazo (pl. los brazos)
back	la espalda*
belly	el vientre/ la barriga/ la pancita *
elbow	el codo*
foot	el pie
hand	la mano
head	la cabeza
knee	la rodilla*
leg	la pierna
stomach	el estómago*

birthday	el cumpleaños
Happy birthday!	¡Feliz cumpleaños!
black	negro (f. negra)
blue	azul
body	el cuerpo
book	el libro
bowl	el tazón
brush (hair)	el cepillo

C

cake	el pastel
candle	la vela
card	la tarjeta
cat	el gato
cereals	los cereales
chair	la silla
cherry	la cereza
chest of drawers	la cómoda
chocolate	el chocolate
clothes	la ropa

✦ ✦ ✦ CLOTHES ✦ ✦ ✦

boots	las botas*
coat	el abrigo*
dress	el vestido
hat	el sombrero
jacket	la chaqueta
jeans	los vaqueros/ los maones*
pants	el pantalón
shirt	la camisa
shoes	los zapatos*
skirt	la falda
socks	las medias*
sweater	el suéter*
T-shirt	la camiseta*

cold	frío (f. fría)
It's cold (weather).	Hace frío.
color	el color

✦ ✦ ✦ COLORS ✦ ✦ ✦

black	negro(a)
blue	azul
brown	marrón*
green	verde
orange	anaranjado(a)*
pink	rosado(a)*
purple	morado(a)*
red	rojo(a)
white	blanco(a)
yellow	amarillo(a)

cookie	la galleta
crocodile	el cocodrilo
to cry	llorar
I'm crying.	Estoy llorando.

D

to dance	*bailar*
I'm dancing.	*Estoy bailando.*
day	*el día*
days of the week	*los días de la semana*

◆ DAYS OF THE WEEK ◆

Monday	*lunes*
Tuesday	*martes*
Wednesday	*miércoles*
Thursday	*jueves*
Friday	*viernes*
Saturday	*sábado*
Sunday	*domingo*

desk	*el escritorio*
die (dice)	*el dado*
dining room	*el comedor*
dog	*el perro*
dolphin	*el delfín*
dress	*el vestido*
duck	*el pato*

E

ear	*la oreja*
eight	*ocho*
eleven	*once*
expressions	*las expresiones*
eyes	*los ojos*

◆ EXPRESSIONS ◆

Hello!	*¡Hola!*
Goodbye!	*¡Adiós!*
Happy birthday!	*¡Feliz cumpleaños!*
Happy New Year!	*¡Feliz año nuevo!**
See you soon!	*¡Hasta la vista!*
Thank you.	*Gracias.*

F

face	*la cara*

◆ THE FACE ◆

cheek	*la mejilla/ el cachete**
chin	*la barbilla/ el mentón**
ear	*la oreja (pl. las orejas)**
eye	*el ojo (pl. los ojos)*
eyebrows	*las cejas**
hair	*el cabello*
lips	*los labios*
mouth	*la boca*
nose	*la nariz*
tooth	*el diente/ los dientes**

fish	*el pez*
five	*cinco*
flower	*la flor*
foot	*el pie*
four	*cuatro*
Friday	*viernes*
frog	*el sapo*
fruit	*la fruta*

◆ FRUITS ◆

apricot	*el albaricoque**
apple	*la manzana*
banana	*el plátano/ el banano*
cherry	*la cereza*
grapes	*las uvas*
lemon	*el limón**
mango	*el mango**
orange	*la naranja**
peach	*el melocotón*
pear	*la pera*
pineapple	*la piña/el ananás**
plum	*la ciruela**
strawberry	*la fresa*

fruit salad	*la ensalada de frutas*
furniture	*los muebles*

◆ FURNITURE ◆

armchair	*la poltrona/ el sillón**
bed	*la cama*
bedside table	*la mesa de noche**
bookcase	*el librero/el estante de libros**
chair	*la silla*
chest of drawers	*la cómoda*
desk	*el escritorio*
lamp	*la lámpara*
shelf	*la repisa**
sofa	*el sofá*
table	*la mesa*

G

gift	*el regalo*
grapes	*las uvas*
green	*verde*

H

hair	*el cabello*
hamster	*el hámster*
hand	*la mano*
happy	*feliz*
Happy birthday!	*¡Feliz cumpleaños!*
hat	*el sombrero*
to have	*tener*
I have . . .	*Yo tengo . . .*
head	*la cabeza*

Hello!	*¡Hola!*
hot	*caliente*
It's hot (weather).	*Hace calor.*
house	*la casa*

◆ AT HOME ◆

attic	*el desván/el ático**
bathroom	*el baño*
bedroom	*el dormitorio*
cellar	*el sótano**
closet	*el ropero**
dining room	*el comedor*
door	*la puerta*
garage	*el garaje**
hall	*el pasillo/ el corredor**
kitchen	*la cocina*
living room	*la sala*
window	*la ventana**

I

I	*Yo*
I am . . .	*Yo soy . . .*
I am . . . years old	*Tengo . . . años.*
in	*en*
in the	*en el/la*
It's cold/hot/nice (weather).	*Hace frío/calor/ buen tiempo.*
It's raining.	*Está lloviendo.*
It's snowing.	*Está nevando.*

J

jacket	*la chaqueta*
to jump	*saltar*
I'm jumping.	*Salto.*

K

kitchen	*la cocina*

L

lamp	*la lámpara*
to laugh	*reír/reírse*
I'm laughing.	*Me río.*
leg	*la pierna*
living room	*la sala*
long	*largo (f. larga)*

M

mask	*la máscara*
mean	*agresivo/desagradable*
Monday	*lunes*
mouth	*la boca*
My name is . . .	*Me llamo . . .*

N

nice	*amable*
nice (weather)	*buen*
It's nice weather.	*Hace buen tiempo.*
nine	*nueve*
no	*no*
nose	*la nariz*

✦ ✦ ✦ NUMBERS ✦ ✦ ✦

one	*uno*
two	*dos*
three	*tres*
four	*cuatro*
five	*cinco*
six	*seis*
seven	*siete*
eight	*ocho*
nine	*nueve*
ten	*diez*
eleven	*once*
twelve	*doce*
twenty	*veinte**
fifty	*cincuenta**
one hundred	*cien**
one thousand	*mil**
one million	*un millón**

number	*el número*

O

one	*uno, una*

P

pants	*el pantalón*
peach	*el melocotón*

✦ ✦ ✦ PETS ✦ ✦ ✦

bird	*el pájaro*
cat	*el gato*
dog	*el perro*
fish	*el pez*
guinea pig	*el conejillo de Indias**
hamster	*el hámster*
kitten	*el gatito**
mouse	*el ratón**
puppy	*el cachorro**
rabbit	*el conejo*
snake	*la culebra**
turtle	*la tortuga*

pear	*la pera*
pen	*la pluma*
pet	*la mascota*
photograph	*la fotografía*
pirate	*el pirata*
plush toy	*el peluche*
princess	*la princesa*

R

rabbit	*el conejo*
to rain	*llover*
It's raining.	*Está lloviendo.*
red	*rojo* (f. *roja*)
remote control	*el control remoto*
round	*redondo* (f. *redonda*)

S

salad	*la ensalada*
Saturday	*el sábado*
seven	*siete*
shark	*el tiburón*
shirt	*la camisa*
short	*corto* (f. *corta*)
Simon says . . .	*Simón dice . . .*
to sing	*cantar*
I'm singing.	*Canto/Estoy cantando.*
six	*seis*
skirt	*la falda*
small	*pequeño* (f. *pequeña*)
soap	*el jabón*
sofa	*el sofá*
to snow	*nevar*
It's snowing.	*Está nevando.*
strawberry	*la fresa*
Sunday	*domingo*
surprise	*la sorpresa*

T

table	*la mesa*
tape	*la cinta*
ten	*diez*
thank you	*gracias*
three	*tres*
Thursday	*jueves*
toothbrush	*el cepillo de dientes*
treasure	*el tesoro*

Tuesday	*martes*
to turn	*dar la vuelta*
I'm turning.	*Doy la vuelta.*
turtle	*la tortuga*
twelve	*doce*
two	*dos*

W

to walk	*caminar*
I'm walking.	*Camino.*

✦ ✦ ✦ WEATHER ✦ ✦ ✦

It's raining.	*Está lloviendo.*
It's nice weather.	*Hace buen tiempo.*
It's hot.	*Hace calor.*
It's cold.	*Hace frío.*
It's snowing.	*Está nevando.*
It's freezing.	*Está helado.**
thunder	*el trueno**
lightning	*el rayo**
rain	*la lluvia**
weather	*el tiempo**

watch	*el reloj*
weather	*el tiempo*
Wednesday	*miércoles*
week	*la semana*
weekend	*el fin de semana*
whale	*la ballena*
white	*blanco* (f. *blanca*)

Y

year	*el año*

✦ ✦ ✦ THE YEAR ✦ ✦ ✦

day	*el día*
hour	*la hora**
month	*el mes**
week	*la semana*
year	*el año**

yellow	*amarillo* (f. *amarilla*)
yes	*sí*